AN AGREEMENT OF THE Free People of England.

Tendered as a *Peace-Offering* to this distressed nation.

BY
Lieutenant Colonel *John Lilburne*, Master *William Walwyn*, Master *Thomas Prince*, and Master *Richard Overton*, Prisoners in the Tower of *London*, *May* the I. 1649.

Matth. 5. verse 9. *Blessed are the Peace-makers for they shall be called the children of God.*

A Preparative to all sorts of people.

IF AFFLICTIONS make men wise, and wisdom direct to happinesse, then certainly this Nation is not far from such a degree therof, as may compare if not far exceed, any part of the world: having for some yeares by-past, drunk deep of the Cup of misery and sorrow. We blesse God our consciences are cleer from adding affliction to affliction, having ever laboured from the beginning, of our publick distractions, to compose and reconcile them: & should esteem it the Crown of all our temporal felicity that yet we might be instrumentall in procuring the peace and prosperity of this Common-wealth the land of our Nativity.

And therefore according to our promise in our late *Manifestation* of the 14 of *Aprill* 1649. (being perswaded of the necessitie and justnesse thereof) as a *Peace-Offering* to the Free people of this Nation, we tender this ensuing Agreement, not knowing any more effectuall means to put a finall period to all our feares and troubles.

It is a way of settlement, though at first much startled at by some in high authority; yet according to the nature of truth, it hath made its own way into the understanding, and taken root in most mens hearts and affections, so that we have reall ground to hope (what ever shall become of us) that our earnest desires and indeavours for good to the people will not altogether be null and frustrate.

The life of all things is in the right use and application, which is not our worke only, but every mans conscience must look to it selfe, and not dreame out more seasons and opportunities. And this we trust will satisfie all ingenuous people that we are not such wilde, irrationall, dangerous Creatures as we have been aspersed to be; This agreement being the ultimate end and full scope of all our desires and intentions concerning the Government of this Nation, and wherein we shall absolutely rest satisfied and acquiesce; nor did we ever give just cause for any to beleeve worse of us by any thing either said or done by us, and which would not in the least be doubted, but that men consider not the interest of those that have so unchristian-like made bold with our good names; but we must bear with men of such interests as are opposite to any part of this Agreement, when neither our Saviour nor his Apostles innocency could stop such mens mouthes whose interests their doctrines and practises did extirpate; And therefore if friends at least would but consider what interest men relate to, whilst they are telling or whispering their aspersions against us, they would find the reason and save us a great deale of labour in clearing our selves, it being a remarkable signe of an ill cause when aspersions supply the place of Arguments.

We blesse God that he hath given us time and hearts to bring it to this issue, what further he hath for us to do is yet only knowne to his wisedom, to whose will and pleasure we shall willingly submit; we have if we look with the eyes of frailty, enemies like the sons of *Anak*, but if with the eyes of faith and confidence in a righteous God and a just cause, we see more with us then against us.

John Lilburn.
William Walwyn.
Thomas Prince.
Richard Overton.

From our causelesse captivity in the Tower of *London, May* 1. 1649.

The Agreement it selfe thus followeth.

After the long and tedious prosecution of a most unnaturall cruell, homebred war, occasioned by divisions and distempers amongst our selves, and those distempers arising from the uncertaintie of our Government, and the exercise of an unlimited or Arbitrary power, by such as have been trusted with Supreme and subordinate Authority, wherby multitudes of grievances and intolerable oppressions have been brought upon us. And finding after eight yeares experience and expectation all indeavours hitherto used, or remedies hitherto applyed, to have encreased rather then diminished our distractions, and that if not speedily prevented our falling againe into factions and divisions, will not only deprive us of the benefit of all those wonderful Victories God hath vouchsafed against such as sought our bondage, but expose us first to poverty and misery, and then to be destroyed by forraigne enemies.

And being earnestly desirous to make a right use of that opportunity God hath given us to make this Nation Free and Happy, to reconcile our differences, and beget a perfect amitie and friendship once more amongst us, that we may stand clear in our consciences before Almighty God, as unbyassed by any corrupt Interest or particular advantages, and manifest to all the world that our indeavours have not proceeded from malice to the persons of any, or enmity against opinions; but in reference to the peace and prosperity of the Common-wealth, and for prevention of like distractions, and removall of all grievances; We the free People of *England*, to whom God hath given hearts, means and opportunity to effect the same, do with submission to his wisdom, in his name, and desiring the equity thereof may be to his praise and glory; Agree to ascertain our Government, to abolish all arbitrary Power, and to set bounds and limits both to our Supreme, and all Subordinate Authority, and remove all known Grievances.

And accordingly do declare and publish to all the world, that we are agreed as followeth,

I. That the Supreme Authority of England and the Territories therewith incorporate, shall be and reside henceforward in a Representative of the People consisting of four hundred persons, but no more; in the choice of whom (according to naturall right) all men of the age of one and twenty yeers and upwards (not being servants, or receiving alms, or having served the late King in Arms or voluntary Contributions) shall have their voices; and be capable of being elected to that Supreme Trust, those who served the King being disabled for ten years onely. All things concerning the distribution of the said four hundred Members proportionable to the respective parts of the Nation, the severall places for Election, the manner of giving and taking of Voyces, with all Circumstances of like nature, tending to the compleating and equall proceedings in

Elections, as also their Salary, is referred to be setled by this present Parliament, in such sort as the next Representative may be in a certain capacity to meet with safety at the time herein expressed: and such circumstances to be made more perfect by future Representatives.

II. That two hundred of the four hundred Members, and not lesse, shall be taken and esteemed for a competent Representative; and the major Voyces present shall be concluding to this Nation. The place of Session, and choice of a Speaker, with other circumstances of that nature, are referred to the care of this and future Representatives.

III. And to the end all publick Officers may be certainly accountable, and no Factions made to maintain corrupt Interests, no Officer of any salary, Forces in Army or Garison, nor any Treasurer or Receiver of publick monies, shall (while such) be elected a Member for any Representative; and if any Lawyer shall at any time be chosen, he shall be uncapable of practice as a Lawyer, during the whole time of that Trust. And for the same reason, and that all persons may be capable of subjection as well as rule.

IIII. That no Member of the present Parliament shall be capable of being elected of the next Representative, nor any Member of any future Representative shall be capable of being chosen for the Representative immediately succeeding: but are free to be chosen, one Representative having intervened: Nor shall any Member of any Representative be made either Receiver, Treasurer, or other Officer during that imployment.

V. That for avoyding the many dangers and inconveniences apparantly arising from the long continuance of the same persons in Authority; We Agree, that this present Parliament shall end the first Wednesday in *August* next 1649, and thenceforth be of no power or Authority: and in the mean time shall order and direct the Election of a new and equall Representative, according to the true intent of this our Agreement: and so as the next Representative may meet and sit in power and Authority as an effectuall Representative upon the day following; namely, the first Thursday of the same *August*, 1649.

VI. We agree, if the present Parliament shall omit to order such Election or Meeting of a new Representative; or shall by any means be hindered from performance of that Trust:

That in such case, we shall for the next Representative proceed in electing thereof in those places, & according to that manner & number formerly accustomed in the choice of

Knights and Burgesses; observing onely the exceptions of such persons from being Electors or Elected, as are mentioned before in the first, third, and fourth Heads of this Agreement: It being most unreasonable that we should either be kept from new, frequent and successive Representatives, or that the supreme Authority should fall into the hands of such as have manifested disaffection to our common Freedom, and endeavoured the bondage of the Nation.

VII. And for prserving the supreme authority from falling into the hands of any whom the people have not, or shall not chuse,

We are resolved and agreed (God willing) that a *new Representative* shall be upon the first *Thursday* in *August* next aforesaid: the ordering and disposing of themselves, as to the choice of a speaker, and the like circumstances, is hereby left to their discretion: But are in the extent and exercise of Power, to follow the direction and rules of this agreement; and are hereby authorised and required according to their best judgements, to set rules for future equall distribution, and election of Members as is herein intended and enjoyned to be done, by the present Parliament.

VIII. And for the preservation of the supreme Authority (in all times) entirely in the hands of such persons only as shal be chosen thereunto—we *agree and declare*: That the next & al future Representatives, shall continue in full power for the space of one whole year: and that the people shall of course, chuse a Parliament once every year so as all the members thereof may be in a capacity to meet, and take place of the foregoing Representative: the first *Thursday* in every *August* for ever if God so please; Also (for the same reason) that the next or any future Representative being met, shall continue their Session day by day without intermission for four monthes at the least; and after that shall be at Liberty to adjourn from two monthes to two months, as they shall see cause untill their yeer be expired, but shall sit no longer then a yeer upon pain of treason to every member that shall exceed that time: and in times of adjurnment shall not erect a Councel of State but refer the managing of affairs in the intervals to a Committee of their own members, giving such instructions, and publish them, as shall in no measure contradict this agreement.

IX. And that none henceforth may be ignorant or doubtful concerning the power of the Supreme authority, and of the affairs, about which the same is to be conversant and exercised: we agree and declare, that the power of Representatives shall extend without the consent or concurrence of any other person or persons,

1. To the conservation of Peace and commerce with forrain Nations.

2. To the preservation of those safe guards, and securities of our lives, limbes, liberties, properties, and estates, contained in the Petition of Right, made and enacted in the third year of the late King.

3. To the raising of moneys, and generally to all things as shall be evidently conducing to those ends, or to the enlargement of our freedom, redress of grievances, and prosperity of the Commonwealth.

For security whereof, having by wofull experience found the prevalence of corrupt interests powerfully inclining most men once entrusted with authority, to pervert the same to their own domination, and to the prejudice of our Peace and Liberties, we therefore further agree and declare.

X. That we do not impower or entrust our said representatives to continue in force, or to make any Lawes, Oaths, or Covenants, whereby to compell by penalties or otherwise any person to any thing in or about matters of faith, Religion or Gods worship or to restrain any person from the profession of his faith, or exercise of Religion according to his Conscience, nothing having caused more distractions, and heart burnings in all ages, then persecution and molestation for matters of Conscience in and about Religion:

XI. We doe not impower them to impresse or constraint any person to serve in war by Sea or Land every mans Conscience being to be satisfied in the justness of that cause wherein he hazards his own life, or may destroy an others.

And for the quieting of all differences, and abolishing of all enmity and rancour, as much as is now possible for us to effect.

XII. We agree, That after the end of this present Parliament, no person shall be questioned for any thing said or done in reference to the late Warres, or publique differences; otherwise then in pursuance of the determinations of the present Parliament, against such as have adhered to the King against the Liberties of the people: And saving that Accomptants for publick moneys received, shall remain accomptable for the same.

XIII. That all priviledges or exemptions of any persons from the Lawes, or from the ordinary course of Legall proceedings, by vertue of any Tenure, Grant, Charter, Patent, Degree, or Birth, or of any place of residence, or refuge, or priviledge of Parliament, shall be henceforth void and null; and the like not to be made nor revived again.

XIIII. We doe not impower them to give judgment upon any ones person or estate, where no Law hath been before provided, nor to give power to any other Court or jurisdiction so to do, Because where there is no Law, there is no transgression, for men or Magistrates to take Cognisance of; neither doe we impower them to intermeddle with the execution of any Law whatsoever.

XV. And that we may remove all long setled Grievances, and thereby as farre as we are able, take away all cause of complaints, and no longer depend upon the uncertain inclination of Parliaments to remove them, nor trouble our selves or them with Petitions after Petitions, as hath been accustomed, without fruit or benefit; and knowing no cause why any should repine at our removall of them, except such as make advantage by their continuance, or are related to some corrupt Interests, which we are not to regard.

We agree and Declare,

XVI. That it shall not be in the power of any Representative, to punish, or cause to be punished, any person or persons for refusing to answer to questions against themselves in Criminall cases.

XVII. That it shall not be in their power, after the end of the next Representative, to continue or constitute any proceedings in Law that shall be longer then Six months in the final determination of any cause past all Appeal, nor to continue the Laws or proceedings therein in any other Language then English, nor to hinder any person or persons from pleading their own Causes, or of making use of whom they please to plead for them.

The reducing of these and other the like provisions of this nature in this Agreement provided, and which could not now in all particulars be perfected by us, is intended by us to be the proper works of faithful Representatives.

XVIII. That it shall not be in their power to continue or make any Laws to abridge or hinder any person or persons, from trading or merchandizing into any place beyond the Seas, where any of this Nation are free to Trade.

XIX. That it shall not be in their power to continue Excise or Customes upon any sort of Food, or any other Goods, Wares, or Commodities, longer then four months after the beginning of the next Representative, being both of them extreme burthensome and oppressive to Trade, and so expensive in the Receipt, as the moneys expended therein (if collected as Subsidies have been) would extend very far towards defraying the publick Charges; and forasmuch as all Moneys to be raised are drawn from the People; such burthensome and chargeable wayes, shall never more be revived, nor shall they raise Moneys by any other ways (after the aforesaid time) but only by an equal rate in the pound upon every reall and personall estate in the Nation.

XX. That it shall not be in their power to make or continue any Law, whereby mens reall or personall estates, or any part thereof, shall be exempted from payment of their debts; or to imprison any person for debt of any nature, it being both unchristian in it self, and no advantage to the Creditors, and both a reproach and prejudice to the Common-wealth.

XXI. That it shall not be in their power to make or continue any Law, for taking away any mans life, except for murther, or other the like hainous offences destructive to humane Society, or for endevouring by force to destroy this our Agreement, but shall use their uttermost endeavour to appoint punishments equall to offences: that so mens Lives, Limbs, Liberties, and estates, may not be liable to be taken away upon trivial or slight occasions as they have been; and shall have speciall care to preserve, all sorts of people from wickedness misery and beggery: nor shall the estate of any capitall offendor be confiscate but in cases of treason only; and in all other capitall offences recompence shall be made to the parties damnified, as well out of the estate of the Malifactor, as by loss of life, according to the conscience of his jury.

XXII. That it shall not be in their power to continue or make any Law, to deprive any person, in case of Tryals for Life, Limb, Liberty, or Estate from the benefit of witnesses on his, or their behalf; nor deprive any person of those priviledges, and liberties, contained in the *Petition of Right*, made in the third yeer of the late King *Charls*.

XXIII. That it shall not be in their power to continue the Grievance of Tithes, longer then to the end of the next Representative; in which time, they shall provide to give reasonable satisfaction to all Impropriators: neither shall they force by penalties or otherwise any person to pay towards the maintenance of any Ministers, who out of conscience cannot submit thereunto.

XXIV. That it shall not be in their power to impose Ministers upon any the respective Parishes, but shall give free liberty to the parishioners of every particular parish, to chuse such as themselves shall approve; and upon such terms, and for such reward, as themselves shall be willing to contribute, or shall contract for. Provided, none be chusers but such as are capable of electing Representatives.

XXV. That it shal not be in their power, to continue or make a law, for any other way of Judgments, or Conviction of life, limb, liberty, or estate, but onely by twelve sworn men of the Neighbor-hood; to be chosen in some free way by the people; to be directed before the end of the next Representative, and not picked and imposed, as hitherto in many places they have been.

XXVI. They shall not disable any person from bearing any office in the Common-wealth, for any opinion or practice in Religion, excepting such as maintain the Popes (or other forraign) Supremacy.

XXVII. That it shal not be in their power to impose any publike officer upon any Counties, Hundreds, Cities, Towns, or Borroughs; but the people capable by this Agreement to chuse Representatives, shall chuse all their publike Officers that are in any kinde to administer the Law for their respective places, for one whole yeer, and no longer, and so from yeer to yeer:

and this as an especial means to avoyd Factions, and Parties.

And that no person may have just cause to complain, by reason of taking away the Excise and Customs, we agree,

XXVIII. That the next, and all future Representatives shall exactly keep the publike Faith, and give ful satisfaction, for all securities, debts, arrears or damages, (justly chargeable) out of the publike Treasury; and shall confirm and make good all just publike Purchases and Contracts that have been, or shall be made; save that the next Representative may confirm or make null in part or in whole, all gifts of Lands, Moneys, Offices, or otherwise made by the present Parliament, to any Member of the House of Commons, or to any of the Lords, or to any of the attendants of either of them.

And for as much as nothing threateneth greater danger to the Common-wealth, then that the Military power should by any means come to be superior to the Civil Authority,

XXLX. We declare and agree, That no Forces shal be raised, but by the Representatives, for the time being; and in raising thereof, that they exactly observe these Rules, namely, That they allot to each particular County, City, Town, and Borrugh, the raising, furnishing, agreeing, and paying of a due proportion, according to the hole number to be levyed; and shall to the Electors of Representatives in each respective place, give Free liberty, to nominate and appoint all Officers appertaining to Regiments, Troops, and Companies, and to remove them as they shall see cause, Reserving to the Representative, the nominating and appointing onely of the General, and all General-Officers; and the ordering, regulatng, and commanding of them all, upon what service shall seem to them necessary for the Safety, Peace, and Freedom of the Common-wealth.

And in as much as we have found by sad experience, That generally men make little or nothing, to innovate in Government, to exceed their time and power in places of trust, to introduce an Arbitrary, and Tyrannical power, and to overturn all things into Anarchy and Confusion, where there are no penalties imposed for such destructive crimes and offences,

XXX. We therefore agree and declare, That it shall not be in the power of any Representative, in any wise, to render up, or give, or take away any part of this Agreement, nor level mens Estates, destroy Propriety, or make all things Common: And if any Representative shall endevor, as a

Representative, to destroy this Agreement, every Member present in the House, not entering or immediately publishing his dissent, shall incur the pain due for High Treason, and be proceeded against accordingly; and if any person or persons, shall by force endevor or contrive, the destruction thereof, each person so doing, shall likewise be dealt withal as in cases of Treason.

And if any person shal by force of Arms disturb Elections of Representatives, he shall incurr the penalty of a Riot; and if any person not capable of being an Elector, or Elected, shal intrude themselves amongst those that are, or any persons shall behave themselves rudely and disorderly, such persons shal be liable to a presentment by a grand Inquest and to an indictment upon misdemeanor; and be fined and otherwise punish'd according to the discretion and verdict of a Jury. And all Laws made, or that shall be made contrary to any part of this Agreement, are hereby made null and void.

Thus, as becometh a free People, thankfull unto God for this blessed opportunity, and desirous to make use thereof to his glory, in taking off every yoak, and removing every burthen, in delivering the captive, and setting the oppressed free; we have in all the particular

Heads forementioned, done as we would be done unto, and as we trust in God will abolish all occasion of offence and discord, and produce the lasting Peace and Prosperity of this Common-wealth: and accordingly do in the sincerity of our hearts and consciences, as in the presence of Almighty God, give cleer testimony of our absolute agreement to all and every part hereof by subscribing our hands thereunto.

Dated the first day of *May*, in the Yeer of our Lord 1649.

John Lilburn.
William Walwyn.
Thomas Prince.
Richard Overton.

April 30. 1649.

Imprimatur.   Gilbert Mabbot

FINIS.

London, Printed for *Gyles Calvert* at the black spread-Eagle at the West end of PAULS.

Made in the USA
Coppell, TX
18 June 2023